The
Connell Short Guide
to
Tennessee Williams's

———

A Streetcar Named Desire

———

by
Kirsten Shepherd-Barr

Contents

NOTES

Introduction

"Streetcar is a cry of pain," Arthur Miller once said, paying tribute to Tennessee Williams's achievement. The most famous line in the play – "I have always depended upon the kindness of strangers" – contains the three most important words for the entire drama. What does it mean to be dependent (or independent)? What does it mean to be kind (or cruel)? And what does it mean to be a stranger? Are we all more or less strangers to one another – even to those we love, and who love us? In a sense, all of Williams's work addresses these fundamental questions, and never more powerfully than in *Streetcar*.

A Streetcar Named Desire was a triumphant success for Williams, running for two years on Broadway (1947-49) and opening in London's West End in 1949. It followed his first hit play, *The Glass Menagerie* (1944). Although they are vastly different in style, the two plays have much in common: their focus on the fragile female and the faded southern belle, their empathy for the marginalised, outcast and oppressed, their emotionally immature male characters, their depiction of the artist figure, their infusion of realism with theatricality and an expressive, poetic language that led critics to hail a new lyricism in a theatre that many felt had grown prosaic and dull. These elements have continued to define Williams as a playwright, despite a much more diverse body of work that is often bravely experimental (e.g. *Camino Real*) and diverges sharply from these early plays. The fact that he is still best known for *Glass Menagerie*, *Streetcar*, and *Cat on a Hot Tin Roof* (1955) is not just because they are enduring and powerful works; it is also due to Hollywood.

The film versions of Williams's plays have stubbornly implanted themselves in the cultural memory through stars like Richard Burton, Marlon Brando, Paul Newman, Elizabeth Taylor and Vivien Leigh, and it is often a great surprise to encounter the plays as they were originally written and discover that the film versions differ radically – most prominently through changed endings that Williams only grudgingly went along with – in ways that deeply affect our interpretations and understanding of the plays. Hollywood gave us indelible individual portrayals, such as Leigh as Blanche DuBois; but it also dampened some of Williams's theatrical ideas and narrowed his range in the public's imagination.

Certain themes do recur in his plays, such as lying, self-deception, human frailty, mental illness, sexual repression, and otherness. But these are not the whole story. Like other great modern playwrights – Ibsen, Chekhov, Strindberg, Beckett – Williams was influenced by two key intellectual developments: psychology and evolution. His works powerfully merge these two strands of thought, exposing with compassion and insight the psychology of character while keeping in focus the larger issue of how environment acts on the individual and the group. *Streetcar* puts these concerns centre stage, asking: how do organisms survive in a hostile environment? Why can't they escape those environments?

A summary of the plot

The play is set in the New Orleans tenement home of Stella, married to Stanley Kowalski and expecting their first baby. Their neighborhood is called Elysian Fields. The play opens with the arrival of Stella's older sister Blanche DuBois, a 30-something former southern belle whose delicate, refined good looks jar with the earthy, steamy, run-down surroundings of the neighborhood where Stella and Stanley live. Her appearance also masks her true situation: she is destitute, having lost the family home, Belle Reve (French for "Beautiful Dream"), to creditors. She has also left her job as an English teacher due, she says, to her nerves. She has come to live with her sister as a last resort. She and Stanley dislike each other from the start, as she finds him "common" and unrefined while he feels she is snooty and intrusive.

Bits of Blanche's past gradually come forth in

the ensuing scenes, as the truth of her circumstances is revealed. She had married very young but was widowed and finds it hard to discuss her dead husband. She confides some of her story to Mitch, a friend of Stanley's who, though he sweats profusely in the sultry New Orleans heat, seems a cut above the other men with whom Stanley plays poker. They flirt. But the evening turns nasty when Stanley, drunk and violent, hits Stella, and she and Blanche flee to the neighbour upstairs, Eunice, who has obviously seen this sort of thing before, while it is a complete shock to Blanche.

Even worse for Blanche, Stella goes back downstairs and to bed with Stanley when he cries out for her repeatedly in the open courtyard. Mitch and Blanche then sit on the front steps and talk about what happened. Mitch apologises for his friend's crass behaviour. The next morning Blanche, assuming that Stella regrets having returned to Stanley after being so badly mistreated by him, tells Stella sympathetically that she regards Stanley as an animal; Stanley overhears this but doesn't let on. Stella shows where her allegiance lies by pointedly hugging and kissing Stanley in front of Blanche.

Tensions mount over the following weeks as Blanche and Stanley continue their frosty stand-off, with no détente in sight. Blanche is nurturing her relationship with Mitch in the hope that she will no longer be a burden for Stella. She reveals to him the truth about her marriage: her husband was gay, as she found out when she discovered him having sex with another man. Blanche told her husband that he disgusted her and he committed suicide.

Mitch is drawn even closer to Blanche by this revelation. But Stanley is trying to undermine her. He has been looking into her past and says to Stella that Blanche was fired from her job as a teacher because she had sex with a student, and lived in a hotel known for prostitution. Stella is so angry and upset by Stanley's viciousness, and for telling Mitch this gossip, that she goes into labour and is rushed to the hospital. Blanche is alone and Mitch comes to confront her. She denies the stories Stanley has told him about her but finally admits they are true. She begs him to forgive her but he spurns her. He seems about to assault/rape her so she screams "fire!" and he flees.

Stanley returns from the hospital, where Stella is expected to deliver the baby by morning. He and Blanche are alone and he apparently rapes her, saying as he carries her into the bedroom: "We've had this date with each other from the beginning." This causes Blanche to have a nervous breakdown and her sister decides to have her committed to a mental institution. Weeks have passed and Stella doesn't believe that Stanley has raped Blanche. Stanley, Mitch and their friends are playing poker when a doctor and nurse arrive to take Blanche away; she fights against them and collapses on the floor, bringing Mitch to tears. The doctor gently helps her to her feet and she goes with him, saying: "Whoever you are, I have always depended upon the kindness of strangers." At the play's close, Stanley is comforting Stella while the poker game goes on.

How Tennessee Williams uses symbolism in *Streetcar*

Two main aspects of *Streetcar* are strongly biographical in nature, and Williams used them repeatedly in his plays. One is the theme of mental illness, particularly that suffered by the fragile female. This is based on Williams's sister Rose, who was given a lobotomy and institutionalised for much of her life. Williams movingly depicts Rose in *The Glass Menagerie* and again in *Streetcar*. The other is the theme of repressed homosexuality. The powerful combination of these themes in so many of his plays makes Williams one of the leading spokesmen of Otherness and oppression.

Fans of *The Glass Menagerie* would have been expecting heavy symbolism in this play too, after their immersion in Williams's magic-realism world of glass figurines, allusions to a unicorn, a broken horn and "blue roses" (pointed symbols of Otherness), the portrait of the deserting father on the walls (the patriarchy), and a brooding narrator-writer revisiting his past on a fire escape (ie. going nowhere). *Streetcar* does not disappoint; even its title, place names and characters breathe symbolic meanings. The opening stage directions evoke all the senses as they describe Elysian Fields, the run-down New Orleans neighborhood permeated by the faint whiff of "bananas and coffee", the feel of the "warm breath of the brown river", the sight of "a peculiarly tender blue" sky, and the sounds of a tinny "blue piano [that] expresses the spirit of the life which goes on here".

Since Elysian Fields is the last stop on the line, the streetcar is paradoxically going nowhere, to a dead end. It also suggests a life lived in transit, yet with no clear destination (or a destination only defined by unfulfilled emotion – desire). The paradox of Blanche arriving in Elysian Fields where her sister lives is clear. In Greek mythology this was the final resting place of the souls of the heroic and the virtuous, and Blanche seems to be neither. As she tells Mitch in their first scene together, Blanche means white and DuBois means woods in French, one of the many languages of New Orleans, a multicultural and linguistic melting pot – or as Williams puts it in the opening stage directions, "a cosmopolitan city" with a "relatively warm and easy intermingling of races in the old part of town". Blanche, by contrast, self-identifies with the woods: a non-urban, dark, solitary environment.

It is common to think of Blanche as a blank white page waiting to be written on. But "to blanch" also means to turn pale, or to turn something else pale, through shock. It has other meanings, too, that all involve unnatural, traumatic or violent processes: in cooking, "to blanch" means to peel by scalding, or to immerse something briefly in boiling water; in botany, it means to whiten a plant by depriving it of light; and in coinage, it describes a method used to whiten metal. Although she pointedly does not flinch when faced with Stanley's rough and overbearing manners during the poker scene, this initial bravado gives way to a scared retreat into the bathroom throughout much of the rest of the play and an increasing sense of being blanched by too harsh an emotional light. How can she survive in the rough environment of Elysian Fields? Far from being the resting place she is seeking, the neighborhood is densely populated, poor, hot and loud from the noise of jazz and streetcars and trains.

As Williams indicates, she looks "incongruous" in this setting, a pure white "moth" fluttering dangerously against the harsh light to which it is inexorably attracted. She has just been seen by both the audience and the men on stage walking in and out of the light, as if flirting with it – although here again we see an interesting contradiction in her as she tells Mitch to attach a lamp-shade to the light because "I can't stand a naked light-bulb". One of Williams's innovations is the way he combines this notion of the light that ruthlessly reveals the truth ("the searchlight turned on the world") with various musical motifs (jazz, polka) to convey Blanche's inner turmoil.

The central scene of the play in which Blanche tells the story about her failed marriage and her husband's suicide, which she directly helped to bring about through her wounding comments ("you disgust me"), expertly interweaves these light and sound motifs. The "searchlight" went off again with his death, Blanche says, and "never for one moment since has there been any light that's stronger than this – kitchen – candle..." When Mitch takes her in his arms, she is speechless; "the words won't come," the stage directions tell us, signalling a brief moment of genuine connection so real for Blanche that it can't be described or expressed.

An added dimension to her character is the theme of cleansing by water; Blanche constantly soaks herself in a hot bath as if to regain her pure-white state, asks if the grapes Eunice has brought are washed, and refers to the cathedral bells as "the only clean thing in the Quarter". She wants to die on the ocean, "be buried at sea sewn up in a clean white sack and dropped overboard". In a very literal sense, her departure for the mental institution at the end of the play suggests that she will have this dream realised in the form of a straitjacket.

The truth about Blanche

"I don't want realism, I want magic," Blanche cries. She is an actress performing a role: that of the elegant Southern belle. The stage directions have her "improvising feverishly" and she does it like a pro. Blanche "lies as a protection against solitude and desperation", says the critic Michael Billington, and her "limitless capacity for self-delusion", a combination of "fake grandeur and genuine pain", is tied explicitly to her gender.

With gestures straight out of a 19th-century melodrama – "she touches her forehead shakily", she speaks with "feverish vivacity", "her knuckles pressed to her lips" – Blanche plays not so much Southern Belle as Lady of the Camellias, and even self-consciously casts herself in this role with Mitch as her lover Armand (scene 6). Given her state of fallenness, some critics have dismissed her as just a "little trollop" (John Chapman), but Harold Clurman saw shrewdly that she was far more than that: she was "the potential artist in all of us". As a woman, she has no stage on which to perform beyond the domestic sphere, so that potential remains untapped and this is what sends her over the edge of sanity. There is a direct line back to Ibsen's heroines, particularly Nora in *A Doll's House*, who likewise performs a role she has learned – how to be female in a male-ordered world – and then realises that she must start again

Gillian Anderson as Blanche DuBois in A Streetcar Named Desire
at The Young Vic in 2014

and learn from scratch, without male instruction and coercion, what it means to be a woman. Nora's frenzied rehearsal of the tarantella dance is often cited as an expression of her extreme mental state brought about by this tension between authenticity and artifice – the moment when she unconsciously shows the impossibility of being herself. Nora and Blanche epitomise this gendered idea of the "theatricalising self". The difference is that Nora comes back from the abyss of insanity while Blanche collapses into it.

Theatre history is full of "mad women": Hamlet's Ophelia is a famous example, and there are many, many others right up to the present day (e.g. in Sarah Kane's *4.48 Psychosis*). Blanche's psychic deterioration is deeply moving, but

Williams shies away from really depicting mental illness; he gives us a hint of what she is going through but doesn't lift the curtain on it. (It's a lot like Ibsen's rather vague depiction of syphilis in his 1881 play *Ghosts*.)

Female playwrights who were near-contemporaries of Williams, like Susan Glaspell and Sophie Treadwell, produced far more vivid and harrowing treatments of "female madness" decades before he did in, respectively, *The Verge* and *Machinal*. And it is a woman, Stella Adler, who most insightfully summarised the character of Blanche. The celebrated acting coach, who worked with Stanislavski and Strasberg, wrote in her performance notes that Blanche, like Amanda Wingfield in *Glass Menagerie*, suffers from the stress of having no profession and no other interest except being a lady. "It has to do with the world of charm or poetry – everything except the realistic world around them. That is their soft, charming world. Some cases have this neurotic clutching on to this sentimentality and dreams and charm because of a conflict within themselves."

Adler's notes illuminate the staging of Blanche's psychological state – that of the floaty, flighty *Southern Belle,* an archetype that fascinated Williams because it belonged to a culture that had, in the words of C.W.E. Bigsby, "jumped the rails of history". Or, as the novelist William Faulkner put it: in the South "the past isn't dead and buried. In fact, it isn't even past" (*Requiem for a Nun*, 1951).

Faulkner's observation certainly explains much about Blanche's entrapment in an outdated social paradigm. But what about her sister; how did she break out of the "southern belle" mould? Blanche describes Stella as "quiet" and "peaceful", full of "beautiful self-control". Stella does indeed seem low-key and compliant; yet her very first words in the play are a command issued to Stanley: "Don't holler at me like that". In many ways she is what Blanche and Stanley are competing for, the object that they both want to possess (both keep calling her "baby"). She consistently acts decisively and firmly in contrast to the uncertain and crumbling Blanche. But her implicit acceptance of Stanley, even though he has just raped her sister, poses a central problem for many readers and viewers.

Novelists have often made sexual violence the hinge of action, leaving it ambiguous as to what actually happens. Thomas Hardy does it in *Tess of the d'Urbervilles*, as does E.M. Forster in *A Passage to India*. It is not so easy to do in the theatre where actions are shown, not narrated. We know exactly what happens between Stanley and Blanche because we see it about to happen and we witness its consequences. How do we react, then, to Stella's implicit forgiveness of Stanley's crime? Is this a weakness of the play, suggesting that Williams held the kind of attitude displayed in playwright John Osborne's statement that "the female must come toppling down to where she should be – on her back. The American male must get his revenge sometime"? Or does it raise uncomfortable questions about human nature when it comes to the complicated workings of love, desire, and trust?

Perhaps the answers lie in the play's broader concern with the workings of human evolution, the potent mix of environment with the forces of change, adaptation and survival. Williams's plays, "while rich in empathy for the defeated, also show an understanding of the instinct for survival" (Michael Billington). Though Blanche claims "I'm very adaptable", it is Stella who is the survivor; she admits that she copes with the knowledge of the rape by suppressing it, just so that she can "go on living". Blanche can see that, and in fact characterises life in evolutionary terms when she calls it a "dark march toward whatever it is we're approaching" and urges Stella not to "hang back with the brutes", alluding to Stanley as "ape-like". Stella herself admits that Stanley belongs to "a different species".

Yet Stanley is not just a simple brute – or, as the critic Harold Bloom rather alarmingly calls him, "amiably brutal" – but a vital bearer of the life force of sexuality "untainted by puritan guilt" (Billington). Bigsby notes that much of *Streetcar*'s shock lay in the fact that, apart from Eugene O'Neill's dramas, "this was the first American play in which sexuality was patently at the core of the lives of all its principal characters". No wonder George Jean Nathan at the time said that *Streetcar* occupied the "shadowy borderline between the unpleasant and the enlightening" and called it – in reference to Brando's hypersexualised performance as Stanley – "The Glands Menagerie".

Sex and violence in the play

A key issue here is the staging of domestic violence. Audiences had just ecstatically welcomed the hit musical *Carousel* (1945) by Rodgers and Hammerstein, a show whose hero is a wife-beating husband. The critical response barely acknowledged that this might be problematic. Two years later, *Streetcar* likewise portrays domestic violence without much protest, as if it's just a part of married life. Even if we don't see all the incidents of violence, we hear them ("There is the sound of a blow. Stella cries out") and we learn that they are part of a continuing chain of abuse. (Eunice hopes they'll "turn the hose on you, same as last time").

Yet Stanley gets away with it every time. Eunice's reprimand – "You can't beat a woman and then call 'er back!....You stinker!" – barely registers as seconds later Stella capitulates to Stanley's cry for her and Mitch brushes aside Stanley's violence:

"don't take it serious," he tells a distraught and confused Blanche, "they're crazy about each other". We also hear domestic violence going on upstairs, with Eunice fleeing her husband Steve to get the police – but this is immediately undercut by Steve emerging with a bruise on his head and the two of them eventually returning in a tight and loving embrace.

Eunice thoroughly approves of Stella's decision to ignore Stanley's rape of Blanche. "Life has got to go on," she says rather lamely, excusing the domestic violence of the men around her. "No matter what happens, you've got to keep on going." As Susan Koprince puts it, Eunice and Steve are the "facsimile of a dysfunctional relationship which normalizes Stanley's abuse". Domestic violence is staged, but it is not fully confronted (as it was, for example, in Opera North's compelling revival of *Carousel* a few years ago). For this reason, in the critic Anca Vlasopolos's view, *Streetcar* is a "problem play" because it remains too ambiguous to provide "ethics" or moral instruction to its audience on these issues, though Philip C. Kolin claims the opposite – that the small part of Eunice signals "complex feminist issues" and draws attention to the plight of battered women.

There is another specifically American context for the play's depiction of a domestic tension that leads to abuse. In 1947, the returning war veterans were coming back to an industrial landscape in which the role of the American male had fundamentally changed. Thomas Adler writes:

> The returning soldier/officer must now be reintegrated into a work force (recently vacated by women whose temporary careers outside the home have been snapped out from under them). The veterans face jobs that are often just as unrewarding and impersonal as the military and a society not yet doing a great deal for those who had served. Their new lives appear closer to drudgery than an opportunity to reap the benefits of the American Dream they fought to preserve and protect.

Elysian Fields seems very far from the American Dream. But how relevant is that concept in the context of this play – how far does it encompass these characters, and their region, its outmoded values, and especially its women? The play's setting is multicultural but only gives us token figures – a drunken and thieving "Negro woman", a blind Mexican woman selling flowers, or the "Polack" Stanley – that never get much beyond stereotype. Perhaps that is exactly Williams's point. He shows us an environment that is rapidly changing: "a culture on the turn... in process of surrendering to a new order" (C.W.E Bigsby).

Williams also suggests that domestic violence is inextricably linked to sexual fulfilment, that these

FIVE FACTS ABOUT
A STREETCAR NAMED DESIRE

1.

A Streetcar Named Desire was originally titled *The Poker Night* but Tennessee Williams changed it after he completed the play in 1946.

2.

So powerful is the legacy of Marlon Brando's protrayal of Stanley Kowalski, the BSL Theatre in Mississippi hosts an annual STELLAAAAA! yelling contest.

3.

Williams changed his name from Thomas to Tennessee (the name of the state in which his father was born) in 1939.

4.

The film of *Streetcar* won four Acadamy Awards in 1951. It won awards for Best Actress, Best Supporting Actor, Best Supporting Actress and Art Direction. Brando lost out to Humphrey Bogart for Best Actor.

5.

Six days before his 28th birthday, Williams was awarded $100 for winning a playwright competition. Entrants had to be 25 or under, but Williams lied about his age – something he was keen to conceal.

Opposite: Marlon Brando and Vivien Leigh in the 1951 film adaptation of A Streetcar Named Desire, *directed by Elia Kazan*

are in fact uncomfortably interdependent. The more intense the sex, the more prone to violence the couples are. Blanche is reputedly just as promiscuous as Stanley, and in fact they are not so different as they initially seem; "they are less victim and villain... than mutual victims of Desire" (Bert Cardullo). Sexuality determines people's futures, often tragically, in so much of American drama: from Eugene O'Neill (*Desire Under the Elms*) and Williams (*The Night of the Iguana, A Streetcar Named Desire, Cat on a Hot Tin Roof, Suddenly Last Summer*) to Edward Albee (*Who's Afraid of Virginia Woolf?*) and Sam Shepard (*Buried Child*). Williams riskily widened the sexual spectrum to encompass greater extremes. His play *The Rose Tattoo* shows a deliriously happy couple who have sex every night, but the point isn't that they are married or that they are heterosexual; sex becomes symbolic and transcendant even while retaining its physicality. Stella and Stanley have a deep and genuine connection through sex; she tells Blanche: "I can hardly stand it when he is away for a night... When he's away for a week I go nearly wild!"

But heterosexual relationships can be repulsive in Williams's plays. Mae and Gooper's big family of "no-neck monsters" in *Cat* is one example (Maggie can hear the two making love like animals through the thin walls); there is also the grossly reproductive, robust, lederhosen-wearing German family in *Night of the Iguana*. Williams is interrogating what is deemed natural sexual behavior. In addition, his plays often hinge on the revelation of some past incident of a sexual nature that has forever blighted the character's life, as in Blanche's aborted marriage to a closeted gay man.

How much does gender matter in *Streetcar*?

Such exaggerated depictions make us ask: how stable are the gender categories Williams represents? The play exuberantly camps up male and female stereotypes. Stanley's "animal joy" is not just sweaty masculinity but is likened to "a richly feathered male bird among hens". Blanche's excessive preening suggests femininity as something performed, stylised, rather than natural. She is often interpreted as symbolising the repressed male homosexual, playing a role and suffering from the same constant state of dishonesty that homosexuality forces on the individual in an intolerant society.

Belle Reprieve (1991), by the lesbian performance group Split Britches (Peggy Shaw, Lois Weaver, Bette Bourne, Precious Pearl), shows how interchangeable the sexual and gender identities in the play can be, and how this is foregrounded through theatrical illusion. *Belle*

Reprieve takes the famous Hollywood film version of *Streetcar* as its starting point and uses vaudeville techniques "to foreground its own performance, suggesting that gender and sexual identification take place at the level of performance", and that there is a "performative dimension" to identity that is "visible even in the repressed mode of American realism" (W.B. Worthen).

The camp aspect to Williams's characters comes through very strongly in the film of *Streetcar*: Marlon Brando's Stanley is savage, primitive, and super-male, Vivien Leigh's Blanche is the fragile, fading Southern belle incarnate. These portrayals are so ingrained in the public consciousness that it is hard to imagine the play without them, which may be why Trevor Nunn's production at the National Theatre in 2002 with Glenn Close as a physically robust, powerful Blanche and Iain Glenn as a wiry and less physically imposing Stanley was not universally admired by critics.

But, as *Belle Reprieve* suggests, maybe Blanche (played by drag queen Bette Bourne) is really an effeminate man; maybe Stanley (played by a swaggeringly butch Peggy Shaw) is really a lesbian; and maybe such categories start to collapse as soon as they are performed. "The pedestrian truth Blanche abhors serves as a metaphor for theatrical realism, while the magic she endorses becomes theatrical experimentation" (Gail Leondar). So often in Williams's plays, just as in his British contemporary Terence Rattigan's, male and female roles are reversible, and heterosexual relationships are thinly veiled homosexual ones. Williams, like Rattigan, had good reason to disguise homosexuality in this way: in America, as in Britain, sodomy was a felony, punishable by imprisonment and/or hard labour.

What the critics say

When the play was first performed, critics were overwhelmingly positive, generally agreeing with The New York Times's Brooks Atkinson that *Streetcar* was "a superb drama... a quietly woven study of intangibles". Praise was heaped on the acting (Jessica Tandy's Blanche and Marlon Brando's Stanley in particular) and on Elia Kazan's direction. Brando made it Stanley's play, whereas later productions emphasised Blanche.

One 1980s's scholar of the play, in fact, maintains that a dichotomy emerges in terms of the characters between reading and seeing it: "audiences favour Stanley, at least in the beginning, while readers favour Blanche" (Roger Boxhill). This chimes with a diagnosis pronounced years earlier by Harold Clurman that "the play becomes the triumph of Stanley Kowalski with the collusion of the audience, which is no longer on the side of the angels". Boxill suggests that one reason for this is the play's use of humour: Stanley gets all the big laughs. Robert F. Gross takes this further, considering key moments in the play and their significance in "forging [the] comic complicity between Stanley and the audience" which has the effect of making Blanche seem amusingly absurd: "in this climate of ridicule, even Blanche's less histrionic moments make the audience laugh... Bereft of delicacy or pathos, the audience reads Blanche's sexual desire as a comic characteristic."

Many commentators were struck by Williams's lyricism and operatic grandness. John Chapman, drama critic for The New York Daily News, called the play "full-scale-throbbingly alive, compassionate, heart-wrenchingly human. It has the tragic overtones of grand opera". Although the play was instantly hailed as a ground-breaking combination of realism and lyricism, some critics felt it was marred by sentimentality. And, on the one hand, *Streetcar* does seem to be the kind of apolitical, family-oriented, sentimental and myopic "diaper drama" that Martin Esslin complained dominated American playwriting. On the other hand, Williams always gestures towards "a larger social and political context that looms forebodingly over the fragile and self-absorbed characters" (W.B. Worthen). Williams himself in an interview provided some insight into his seeming lack of engagement with contemporary political issues: when asked why he didn't write overtly about Civil

Rights, he replied:

> I always try to write obliquely... I am not a direct
> writer; I am always an oblique writer, if I can be; I
> want to be allusive; I don't want to be one of these
> people who hit the nail on the head all the time.

How innovative was Tennessee Williams?

American drama in the period focused on plot and
the nuts and bolts of dramaturgy. Athur Miller
complained that playwriting was "regarded as
something close to engineering, structure and its
problems taking first place in all considerations of
the art... Williams [by contrast] had pushed
language and character to the front of the stage as
never before." It's a great irony that Williams has
been perceived as a master realist when in fact
throughout his career he experimented constantly
with non-realistic forms.

He named Chekhov and Strindberg as key
influences; he called himself a Symbolist; he used
Brechtian devices; he played with elements of
incongruity and the grotesque, as in the subtle
stage directions to *Cat on a Hot Tin Roof* that call
for a disproportionately large bed and drinks
cabinet in Maggie and Brick's otherwise realistic

bedroom. He also made thoughtful contributions to theatre theory in his reflections on the craft in such essays as "The Timeless World of the Play", which stand alongside Miller's essays on theatre.

The critic Harold Bloom intones that "the fall of Blanche is a parable, not of American civilization's lost nobility, but of the failure of the American literary imagination to rise above its recent myths of recurrent defeat". The South is one such myth in Williams's play. But such stentorian pronouncements often overlook other aspects of the play, such as the innovative use Williams makes of poetry, art, and music. Williams's vision of theatre draws especially from the world of visual art. For example, in the opening stage directions to Scene Three (the poker game), he invokes Van Gogh's painting of a billiard-parlor at night, with its "lurid nocturnal brilliance" and "raw colors".

Van Gogh's art is a fitting analogy with Williams's own approach, showing realistic surroundings in an impressionist style in which it is more important to convey an idea or a sense of a place, an atmosphere, than to aim at faithful photographic replication. Throughout the play there is an emphasis on bright, strong, vivid colour, especially red, blue and yellow – the primary colours. Surprisingly Blanche herself asserts that she prefers these shades, contrary to the association we often make of her with all things pale and white.

It is significant that the French translator of *Streetcar* was the Surrealist writer Jean Cocteau. This fits with Williams's own emphasis on style as "the substance, not just the veneer, of a work of art" (Marc Robinson). The scene when Blanche is alone with Stanley, he is becoming increasingly menacing and her nerves are collapsing exemplifies Williams's surrealism:

> *Lurid reflections appear on the walls around Blanche. The shadows are of a grotesque and menacing form....The night is filled with inhuman voices like cries in a jungle. The shadows and lurid reflections move sinuously as flames along the wall spaces.*

Then suddenly the back walls of the room become transparent. As she cowers in the corner, Stanley advances on her with his tongue "protruding between his lips," the "blue piano" softly playing in the background, and the "inhuman jungle voices" rising up. Williams later signals Blanche's total breakdown by having these "lurid reflections" reappear, now accompanied by "mysterious voices behind the walls, as if reverberated through a canyon of rock". This time it is not Stanley but the burly matron who advances to pin her down.

Theatre by its very nature tells lies; we are expected to suspend our disbelief, as Coleridge instructed, or else we would simply get up and leave. What C.W.E. Bigsby calls "the theatricalising self" is everywhere in Williams's work, giving a direct link between the genre of theatre and the themes he explores. In fact, Marc Robinson goes further and argues that Williams has a "scepticism, if not openly embarrassed antitheatricalism" (270). In *Glass Menagerie* he "conducts a withering, if largely implicit, critique of his medium, indicting it for an inability to sustain illusion, reflect the flux of real life, and gratify the imaginative longings of both playwright and spectator". The play's many destructive moments "stand in for renunciations Williams himself can't make against an art that betrays its promise" to deliver these things to its audience. *Streetcar* provides a perfect example of a theatrical melding of form and content that both recognises, yet at the same time seeks to destabilise, its own medium.

This idea of betrayal ultimately provides the key to why Blanche ends up relying on strangers, and finding them "kind", for she has been betrayed by her own family and friends and by the illusions she has created about her relationships with them. Stella delivers her sister to the insane asylum, without telling her the truth about where she is going. While this takes a toll on Stella, who is clearly devastated by guilt, the play's ending suggests that life will go on; as the lights come down she and Stanley embrace and he is unbuttoning her blouse. Meanwhile, Mitch is "sobbing" over Blanche's tragic departure – a poignant but fairly useless emotional response to her plight as it does nothing whatsoever for Blanche. In the face of such treatment, her shift at the end of the play from reliance on the familiar to reliance on strangers is inevitable, and is her only way out apart from death.

In 1957, Williams wrote an interview with himself called "The World I Live in" (published in the London Observer) in which he spelled out his "message". He said he wrote plays in order to dramatise

> the crying, almost screaming, need of a great worldwide human effort to know ourselves and each other a great deal better, well enough to concede that no man has a monopoly on right or virtue any more than any man has a corner on duplicity and evil and so forth.

He said he didn't understand why we are always being taught "to hate and fear other people on the same little world that we live in. Why don't we meet these people and get to know them as I try to meet and know people in my plays?" In addition to echoing almost verbatim a song from the hit musical *South Pacific* (1949), which inveighs against a society that teaches us "to hate and fear" people with different eyes and skin colour,

Williams here speaks eloquently about the concept of "strangers" as it applies to his play *Streetcar*. Again the keynote here is the breaking down of barriers between people, a process that is exactly the reverse of what we see happening in *Streetcar* as, coping with a confusing world in which the familiar is more threatening and duplicitous than the unknown, Blanche erects barriers (retreating into the bathroom, for instance, or telling lies about her past) between herself and those she knows, finally fleeing to the unknown and the "kindness of strangers". Her story is in many ways an enactment of Williams's own lifelong attempts through his writing to break down the inculcated "hate and fear" he found so endemic to American culture and society.

A SHORT CHRONOLOGY

1911 March 26 Thomas Lanier Williams is born in Columbus, Mississippi

1929 - 1931 Williams attends the University of Missouri

1944 *The Glass Menagerie*

1947 December 3 *A Streetcar Named Desire* premieres on Broadway

1948 *Streetcar* wins the Pulitzer Prize for Drama

1951 *Streetcar* film adaptation

1955 *Cat on a Hot Tin Roof*

1959 *Sweet Bird of Youth*

1983 February 24 Tennessee Williams dies in New York City

FURTHER READING

Thomas Adler, *Streetcar: The Moth and the Lantern* (1990)

C.W.E. Bigsby, *Modern American Drama, 1945-1990* (1992)

Michael Billington, *State of the Nation* (Faber, 2007)

Michael Billington, *The 101 Greatest Plays* (Faber, 2015)

Harold Bloom, ed., *Modern Critical Views: Tennessee Williams's A Streetcar Named Desire* (2009)

Roger Boxhill, in *Macmillan Modern Dramatists: TW*, 1987, p. 80

Bert Cardullo, "Birth and Death in *A Streetcar Named Desire*," in Philip C. Kolin, ed., *Confronting Tennessee Williams's A Streetcar Named Desire: Essays in Critical Pluralism* (1993)

Alan Chesler, *Streetcar: Twenty Five Years of Criticism* (1973)

Harold Clurman, *The Collected Works of Harold Clurman: Six Decades of Commentary on Theatre, Dance, Music, Film, Arts, and Letters* (1994)

Robert F. Gross, "Hello Stanley, Good-bye Blanche: The Brutal Asymmetries of Desire in Production"

Philip C. Kolin, *Tennessee Williams: A Guide to*

Research and Performance (1998)

Philip C. Kolin, ed., *Confronting Tennessee Williams's A Streetcar Named Desire: Essays in Critical Pluralism* (1993)

Susan Koprince, "Domestic Violence in *A Streetcar Named Desire*," in Harold Bloom, ed., *Tennessee Williams's A Streetcar Named Desire* (2009)

Brenda Murphy, *Tennessee Williams and Elia Kazan: A Collaboration in the Theatre* (1992)

Brenda Murphy, ed., *The Theatre of Tennessee Williams* (2014)

Jacqueline O'Connor, *Dramatizing Dementia: Madness in the Plays of Tennessee Williams*

Marc Robinson, *The American Play* (2009)

Kirsten E. Shepherd-Barr, *Theatre and Evolution from Ibsen to Beckett* (2015)

Stephen Sadler Stanton, ed., *Tennessee Williams: A Collection of Critical Essays* (1977)

Anca Vlasopolos, "Authorizing History: Victimization in *A Streetcar Named Desire*," in *Feminist Rereadings of Modern American Drama*, ed. June Schlueter, pp. 149-70.

Katherine Weiss, *A Student Handbook to the Plays of Tennessee Williams* (2014)

W.B. Worthen, *Modern Drama: Plays/Criticism/Theory* (1995)

Notes

Notes

Notes

Notes

I'd like to thank my research assistant, Ciarán Clibbens, for his invaluable help in preparing the volume.

First published in 2016 by
Connell Guides
Artist House
35 Little Russell Street
London WC1A 2HH

10 9 8 7 6 5 4 3 2 1

Picture credits:

p.11 © REX Features
p.19 © Alamy

A CIP catalogue record for this book is available from the British Library.
ISBN 978-1-907776-94-6

Design © Nathan Burton
Written by Kirsten Shepherd-Barr
Edited by Jolyon Connell

Assistant Editors and typeset by
Paul Woodward and Holly Bruce

www.connellguides.com